To
DIL FAREB

TO

RICHARDSON

CONTENTS

The Solitudes

Other Poems

THE SOLITUDES

I

To my essential self—I sing—
Not to the I,
Man of the hat, coat and tie;
But to the me,
—coffee, muddle and misery.

2

Damn and blast you!
You behave like a pickpocket,
    or an absent-minded thief,
Raiding my sleep, when you don't even need my peace;
Stealing my heart, when you certainly don't want my
    love.

And all this done so bloody gracefully,
Done out of perversity, done out of sheer caprice,
Till I am undone, utterly besotted.

True, it's not your fault, you're not to blame:
Your sleight of hand's so practised, you don't even know
    you do it
And can't even think who it is
    who now complains bitterly—
    because of his anonymity.

I tell you beauty like yours should be punishable.
What right have your eyes to run up and down the street,
    creating this disturbance?
Your breasts are urchins; your lips, ragamuffins;
Everything about you is delinquent,
The whole of you gangs up
    to chuck pebbles through my fragile maturity.

But one day, madam, I'll read the Riot Act to your thighs,
And claim back all my property, bit by bit, till I am whole
    again.

Till then, do not reform,
Treat me as an unguarded barrow loaded high with
     grapes,
    or an unstaffed stocking store,
Snaffle my peace of mind, knock off my capacity to
     work,
As for my reputation, I value nothing which you do not
     take;
    Nor want these rags, the remnants which you leave.

3

To the lake of my aloneness
    No river flows
I am contained by mountains of my making.
Without wave I wait, wanting; but no heron
    comes and no swan goes.
The day delivers its indifferent glances;
Night passes, merely pausing to adjust
    an artificial rose.
I hold nothing but reflections;
I wake to my own shallows, I sleep soundly
    without repose.
Will no appled boy paddle in me?
Or sunlaced girl dive and swim in me?
Has no one a boat to float on me?
Must I to quench my thirst, drink myself up
    and drown?

4

I would that my love should grow
    without a heart to feed upon;

I would that my heart should feed
    without a life to lean upon;

I would that my love should shine
    without an object, without a shadow;

I would that I should die within myself
    and live in my love for you and you and you
    as He did, yielding without possessing;
All other love is death,
    is death's amorous dissembling.

5

How leaf we are;
    At first, all furled in separateness:
Peeping out with little vanities and hopes, also vanity;
Perhaps the last vanity, holding us to that green world
Our life shall be; believing ourselves
    So individual, we all reach, being identical.
Shall the prodigal gardener weep?

How leaf we are;
    At last, all seared in brittleness
Curled up with tiny fears and hurts, also fears;
Perhaps the last fear, tethering us to that dry twig
Our life's become; then knowing that we are
    Enumerable, we fall, being expendable, all.
The gardener is blind. He will not sweep.

How leaf we are
    Like waves we do become; first urged, then merged.
That gardener is a fisherman;
That fisherman's asleep.

6

Why do You
    laugh up Your sleeve of night
    watching me, lonely, without You,
    knowing You did not give me the sight to see You,
    nor the strength to seek You?

What perverse pleasure do You find
    playing cat and mouse and hiding from the blind
    teasing the already torn and tormented mind?

And tell me: why did You have to give me eyes
    which can only stare at her
    and do not even glance at Thee?
    Why did You lame me so
    That I can run—to her
    And cannot come—to Thee?

Cannot your divine and imprudent purpose be fulfilled
Unless I deny Thee so that You in Your turn can then,
        forgive me?
Is my weakness indispensable to your strength?
Are we tied together—a tin can to a dog's tail?
It must be or You would not have made me so
    That I can kneel to her
    And will not bend to Thee;
    That I can reach for her,
    And cannot rise to Thee.

Or is it—oh, be it so—
    That Thou made her for me
    Knowing that by loving her, I'd come to Thee,
    finding in her hands, Thy gentleness;
    On her lips, Thy tenderness;
    In her passion, Thy compassion?

It is so—oh do not take her from me—
    for see, Jesu, how I now run gaily to her, to Thee,
    Making this prayer a song to her, to Thee,
    an avowal without heresy.
    For as you know, Christ how well you know,
    When only love divides,
    Nothing is divided.

7

As wet lilac bruised with scent
Leans on the air indolent
And allows the wind to break
And permits the sun to slake
Its fierce thirst and quietus make

So you, my love, allow
And give, and add to it your vows
But do not seek a pledge from me.
Your vows give me my liberty,
Your eyes describe my tyranny.

8

You ask me to write a poem
Not because you like poetry
But because you like me,
And want to give something to me.

But because you are humble
(Modesty is another thing)
You do not offer me yourself, but myself
Knowing that is what I have lost or
                          absentmindedly mislaid,
And that it is something I shall not find again
In her, or her or you.
But might in moments like this to which you lead me
When I sit fishing in silence from a shoal of
                          quicksilver words
Which leap like salmon the instant that I look.
It does not matter where I look
      at the petals of lilac falling to the grateful lawn;
      at the tractor trailer burdened with its load of dung;
      at her, or her or even you . . . it does not matter,
Anything which lives is poetry.

The restless swallows dive for flies, hunger is their song;
Watching them, I am, I find that self whenever I do not
          belong.
So now I can give you this,
                          the self you give to me.

9

Because my eyes have stared
　　　So often at you
People looking at me
Should see your image impaled upon my face.

IO

Dearest, do me a favour
　　　Treat me without mercy;
Let your cruelty
　　　　Run free, so long as it runs over me
Love me as the wind loves
Waste me as water is wasted;
Ask and demand all from me, take the whole of
　　me;
For only when you take that
　　　Can you give me, me.

11

Now that we love
        watch how the world conspires
To wreck, ruin and upset
        this raft of our desires;
Now that we love
        observe how Time will cheat
Us of that coinage
        we do not counterfeit;
Yet now that we love
        restrain all tears, just laugh;
Let joy be our purpose
        a smile, our epitaph.

12

Dearest, since I cannot say why I love you
Let me tell you how I love you:
    I love you as a tiger loves its prey,
        intently, fiercely;
    I love you as the ivy loves its wall,
        closely, tenaciously;
    I love you as the lizard loves the sun
        completely, sleepily;
Dearest, if I must live without you,
It will not be life without you.
    Those who are born only once, die only once;
That is not our fate. But I am content in:
    the mercy of your being.

13

How can we be parted
Since we are no longer separate?
The train that conspires to take me from you
Will only take me to you:
You will be on the platform to greet me,
You will be in the taxi beside me.
Though I may speak to others,
I shall be talking to you;
Though I may look at others
I shall be looking for you.
When I walk I shall be walking towards you,
When I sleep I shall be lying beside you.
Because we are no longer separate
We cannot be parted. Yet I dread the world
That does not hold your eyes.

14

Dearest, it is no longer true
  For me to say I love you
Or that I desire you, though that was true
    A day or two ago, before you took me to yourself
      And from an individuality
      Made one identity
  To which we each are part and now belong.

For me to say I love,
Or that I still desired you
    Would be as tautological
    as tactful,
  For we are in that state
  In which there is no predicate or object.
  Those who are separate
                love at lower rate.

15

Her moss of sleep upon the bark of night,
Her surf of dreams upon the tide of rest;
      So do we lie;
The lark of now into the song of sky;
Our leaf of love upon the tree of time;
      The wind blows, my blind hand knows
Sight, touching her breast.

16

As thrush, lark and linnet are
    So do my eyes rise,
Sing for the life in you
    Joyful at your being. Oh
                be there

Where I am going, when I return to
    Be bark to my ivy
Tree to my climbing
    Be merciful
                be here

Where my hope is, be there where my home was,
    Else I am lost, lonely as driftwood;
Be to the restless river, me
    Clear pool of no purpose
                be still

Peaceful as grass is, grow gently,
    Secretly beneath
Impetuous rain of me
    Be brave at my cruelty
                believe

In my gentleness; forgive me for this,
    Forgive me for that. Contain my disparities;
Accept my extremities. Oh love me wholly, so
    Holy shall you
                become.

All right, run off with you and go
But let me warn you, Madam, where you go, I am.
    The more you run from me,
    The more you run to me,
What you become, I am.

You seek another lover? Oh don't deny, or lie;
That's a useless thing to do to him
Who's made all these frailties his own.

But let me ask you: what quality has any other man
        Except he is not me,—
A somewhat negative attribute, you agree?

All he could be at his poor best
Would be to be deputy, understudy,
Plagiarising my hands, aping my eyes, parodying my lips,
And it's you who'll cast him as this stand in
To watch him try what I alone perform.

But I'm not jealous, give him encouragement, it's all
        you'll yield.
And all he'll take from you will be your tolerance,
Your patience and a yawn.

And don't think I'm being arrogant
I don't despise him. You misunderstand me there:
It is that I, being so sympathetic to his role
Am, he, at one remove.

And don't apologise; I have reached that point, philo-
  sophically,
   Where I perceive all lovers only labour and perform
     for me;
Extended thus, spiritually,
Insulated so, emotionally, I achieve
   Both the ease you denied me
And the anonymity that is yours.

18

There was no part of you
    my hands did not know.
Now separated,
    let the memory of my hands
Enfold your neck, your breasts, your thighs,
    gentle as petals fall
    or the wings of butterflies rise.

Be like a chrysalis contained by my fingers, encased by
            my touch:
Let the rude world stare at this robe you wear
    Dior could not copy it
    Paquin imitate it;
Go dressed in my hands, my desire the designer
    Clothed in this passion
    You are the height of fashion.

So flaunt the memory of my hands proudly
Till this blind glove with which I now write
Can undress you, and from your nakedness
Receive its flesh, its purpose and its sight,
Embroidering your skin in the fierce tattoo of night.

19

Oh my God with what agility
does jealousy
             jump into a hot heart
and fit,
      till it fills it,
             or is, a great part.

And how strange it is that I myself
should from myself
            make, riding her thighs
at speed
      (or slow as love needs),
              rivals which are his eyes

Unfocussed, yet in blindness seeing
all of being;
         opaque, his opal eyes shew
sorrow,
     it is as though,
            my wrinkled son had said:
'I who am born was never dead' and said:

'There is no birth, death, joy or sorrow
I am not you,
        nor are you me;
we are each free,
        linked with no separate identity.

All is as water flowing endlessly
leisurely
        over a smooth hard stone.
Only a thin skin,
           pattern on the water, this, our own.'

Do me a favour, treat me with contempt:
  Laugh at my poetry, say my last play's dull, a bore,
Not half as good as one I wrote before.
  Find where my faith hides and what my ideals are—
or were, then ridicule them. Beg for my heart
  And when I give it you
  Bounce it casually on the floor—
                    No more!
    That's not enough! Do more!

Make lonely my own home: rid me of sleep,
  And if and when I do, play patience with my dreams,
Shuffle dexterously, mark the whole pack;
  And when I wake, see that it's not from you.
Cheat me of purpose; deprive me of my wit,
  Make me despise myself
Assure all my friends' derision—
                    No more!
    That's not enough! Do more!

Cuckold me with a painter—anyone will do
  For me, or you! Inform me of the day, the hour, the place
Make sure I hear the details—tell her
  In secret, leave the salt to her: omit no item
Or dimension; do as all bitches do—
    exaggerate one or two
    brag it was better than before
                    No more!
    That's not enough! Try more!

Find where I'm vulnerable, then stretch the wound.
   Borrow my money—there's an idea for you!
Try breaking my pocket since my pride won't break
   Then when I need the cash, say you gave it him!
You'd think that ruse would work, but if it fails:
   Promise to dine with me; come late
                No more!
   That's not enough! Much more!

Make me complain, then say you'll give him up,
   Swear vows or try at least to produce a tear or two
Till I, to stop the flow, beg you to forgive
   Me—for making you do what you did to me.
Now comes your chance; reconciled and grateful
  I drop all my defence
   Aim straight, wound where I am still raw
                No more!
   That's not enough! Do more!

Betray me utterly. For that you'll need
   Some new device; a mere fuck or two won't do.
Even when you admit that lapse was not
   From weakness but deliberately done:
That your vow was false as the groans you faked
   for him. No any cunt
   Can do that trick. Try something more:
                Much more!
   It's not enough! Do more!

What could it be? Where is a poet hurt?
   Ponder a while—what's made 'em bleed like hell
     before?

When digs into their pride and pocket failed?
   What drove da Falla mad, made Minton drink
Pushed poor Van Gogh till he removed an ear—
   Or was it something else
   Or more? You'd know if it were that!
                          Think more!
   That's not enough! Think more!

Think what it was bust Schubert's mighty heart
   That's it. You're getting close! You're getting warm,
      I see!
Yes; we all share the same sincerity.
   So hunt out some token which I gave to you
Sell it. Tell what I told you through my eyes
   In secret. Play it down.
Not just the moment, cheapen me
                     No more!
   You've tried all that! Get more!

Get dentures loose, then henna up your hair.
   Deflate your breasts, achieve a spotted thigh, be smug,
Be slovenly in your dress, shifty in your eye
   Acquire indifference. Oh, for pity's sake,
Do these things which time will do to you—
   For all the rest you've done
      Yet I still love, as I have loved before
                  It's not enough?
   Find more! Find more!

21

Murderers are merciful compared to me
   who with the same intention
   lacked their resolution
And failed, but not from kindness, I was never without
       cruelty
That you know; nor was it that I had no need, that I know;
For my peace, I had to put you to rest,
                 And so I tried
Several slow ways to kill you,
                    yet you have not died.

You will remember my first attempt
   which lacked a dagger's courage
   or a poison's quick relief:
How I struck blindly where you were most vulnerable,
At your love, and where I knew you were undefended,
       because you loved.
I did not use a knife; my words were sharper
                As I denied
My love and watched my words wound and saw you
       bleed
                    yet you have not died.

And at that failure, how I next sought
   to strangle what I'd weakened
   though it had not died, though I then sent you from
       me
And told her, and her and him that you meant nothing
       to me
Knowing they from friendship would tell you. . . .

Christ! how I lied
And tried to hide the wound you were that blossomed in
　　　my side
　　　　　　　　　yet you have not died.

But out of perversity you have grown stronger
　　　as though you fed upon neglect
　　　and were nourished by starvation;
And so, at last, I brought you back again to see if famili-
　　　arity would kill
What had only flourished when we parted. And how I
　　　next
Belittled what you gave me, and urged myself to con-
　　　tinence
　　　　　　　　　till you complied
And let me be as faithful to her as you remained to me,
　　　　　　　　　yet you have not died.

Even though I then drove you to another
　　　Hoping jealousy might do for me
　　　What it had failed to do for you;
And how I then used to come and sit upon the bed where
　　　you had lain—
　　　　　　　　　or should I say had lied?
Yet savoured your betrayal
　　　　　　　　　pretending we were identified,
Managing to absolve myself of responsibility to you
　　　　　　　　　yet you have not died.

But have become the mongrel at my side
　　　I run from only to seek;
　　　As a blind man, his guide,

37

So on you I relied; not for my existence, but for my being.
Of what use were my eyes unless they saw you? My hands
Unless they touched you? . . . That dependence
                              I abhorred, defied
And deliberately tried to hide from that unwanted bitch
          that dogged my side
                              yet you have not died.

But lived a restful life within my restless sleep
          So that all my dreams were webs
          To catch you on the wing,
Or like busy streams pretending to turn from you
Only to flow to you. Peace was where you were, and you
                    were in my sleep
As I'm in yours. . . . Thus do we two lie apart, but not
          alone, certainly not divided
                              As night's tide
Turns and makes us wake to loneliness
                              Yet you have not died.

Though I have sought within this wilderness of thought
          To murder what I loved,
          Knowing that was suicide,
For we are what we love; but not mercy, self-survival
Now makes me keep you and your memory alive in me.
          And now I have lain you in this verse
Live there after your life in me
                              when I have died
For, till then, there is no way
                    for you to die in me—though I have tried,
                              though you have tried.

22

If our ability to love
Can only be assessed by our capability to forgive, then
        my darling,
I must be grateful to you for teaching me the language,
Though I confess I've sometimes found it difficult
To articulate all the charity you earned
And was till now often dumb with resentment, bankrupt
        in my love.

The fault was yours; how could I learn to forgive
If you failed to confess? I blame you there,
Your modesty and reticence made me backward
And my Elementary Love remained in the Remove,
Not knowing the tenses of maturity
Or the conjugations of your sex.

How could my love develop, if it
Had so little to forgive, and I was always the one
To be forgiven? No wonder I remained
Still learning the alphabet
While you graduated from tolerance to indifference.

It was not kind of you to keep me illiterate for so long.
Knowing your virtue, taught me nothing but that I
        lacked it.
True, I admired you for yours; but since I thought you
        faithful to me,
Your virtue was something I left for others to forgive.

If I've been jealous it was because
I thought you were giving them lessons you denied to me.
That this was not the case, and they had nothing to for-
give
Does not alter the fact that I now sit here for my ex-
amination
Without having had adequate preparation.

Your little perjuries were not enough
To teach me charity. Neither were your fits of envy
—I mean those of me—sufficient for my education;
Nor was your frigidity a fault to teach me
Anything but pity; and pity has no more to do with love
Than desire has with compassion.

You were of course quite generous to me
In your long deception: I thank you for that.
For if you had told me frankly at the time
That you had been unfaithful to me
I would have had nothing to forgive—
Except that more temptation had come to your door
Than I had often found in my gutter.

No, it was not your long deception
That is my present lesson. That's too easily understood,
Too easily forgiven. It's one thing to tell a priest—
But a husband tends to be more attentive
And less impartial as a confessor.

Besides which, as I know we sometimes
Hide the truth from those we love, not for our own
protection,

40

But for theirs. That you did this to me,
Was no more than to quote me to my face;
And though I tend to resent my own faults seen in others,
—plagiarism flatters as the devil only knows.

And of course women have their own temerity,
They can't brag of their adulteries with effrontery,
They have to be secret in order to be kind; as Sweeny
        says:
Somebody has to pay the rent; and as that's not them
What else can they do but go on nourishing their in-
        discretion?
Though the worm gnaws at their breast, they can always
        wear a bra.

No, your lies and adulteries give me as little to forgive
As your insensitivity did—or does.
And, of course, I know you would have been more
        honest
If I had been more understanding. To condemn a woman
        for her lies
Is as unreasonable as blaming a bird for its wings.
The best we could do would be to resent the fact that
        their flight
Is always more sustained than ours.

Similarly, I realise that you would have been more
        faithful
If faith had been more fashionable. And was I not
A leader of fashion—we'll not refer to taste?

For there to be forgiveness, there must be anger first;
And the more I hear, the more sympathy obtrudes.
Now what can I learn of love, if I've only fashion to
 forgive?

Even if you'd used your pretence of virtue
To double my sense of guilt, so that I had then become
Untrue to myself, as I had been untrue to you,
And if that had then made me abandon her
And loose my self-respect—even that I could easily
 forgive.

For when a woman helps a man to loose all self-esteem
She does him a greater favour than she knows
Or maybe she intends. Yes, even if you had done this to
 me
And made me lose a woman's love, that would have been
 a favour,
Certainly, nothing I could not forgive.

You claim that's what you did? Then it seems you are
 forgiven—
Poets, my darling, are born with love. I did not need
 your lesson.

Any man might miss
    Your lips or thighs, but I
Miss the slut, the shrew in you;
And hate this quiet peace which lacks your nasty tongue,
Bored with my bed too big without your bum.

Any man might want
    You for your charm, but I
Want the bitch, the nag of you;
And walk this slow evening so dull without your spite,
Sick of my thought, less you're distracting it.

Any man might love
    You for some part, but I
Love you whole, even your heart,
In which I am contained, though I've not entered it,
—Or so you say sometimes, only because you wish to
       give it me again.

24

Just as I used
    to wear your old sweater
Preferring the rag that was yours
    because it was yours
to anything that was mine,

So now I wrap myself
    within this loneliness
Preferring this fact and its cause
    because it is yours
to any dream that was mine.

25

I have at last come to terms
    with your curtains;
I can now look at them for what they are;
They no longer hurt me because you made them.

And slowly I am making my peace
    with your garden.
I see your bulbs now like fingers through the weeds
They make me sad, but it is a sadness I am learning to
      accept.

It is your pile of flat stones
    by the gate;
Those you dragged bravely up from the bed of the stream
To make a path with, it is that which is so belligerent
      and will have me on the run.

26

Dearest, be ruthless:
    give me more love
Or give me more disdain;
Abandon your pose of pity,
Stop teasing me, show me contempt;
Love of our intensity
                    should be violent to be tender:
It's your kindness that is unkind.

Dearest, be generous
    give me more love
Or give me more despair
Either yourself or your emnity:
Stop liking me, be cruel and hate;
Love of our intensity
                    should be savage to be gentle;
It's your kindness that is unkind.

27

Words are a net;
Feeling, the water escapes through the meshes
I fish for silence.

OTHER POEMS

D

OTHER POEMS

THE NEED
(Birthday poem for Rose Marie)

At twenty
    you were the distraction
I concentrated on:
At thirty
    you were the meditation
which I brooded upon;
At forty
    you are the temptation
I will not resist.
    Time makes its creases
But your loveliness increases.
Youth is but a bone which years dress
with something more durable than flesh.
Wear your summers proudly,
Flaunt your winters too.
Put your age on gaily like a scarf.
Forty Aprils lie behind your eyes;
In them I see all May's squandered treasury;
In them I'll look in your autumn, for my autumn.
My eyes are blind unless it's yours they see.
You doubt me? True, you are too old for flattery,
Too young for vanity. What then can I give you
As an appropriate present? Diamonds are too cheap,
Furs tawdry; money would profane.
No, I will give you something
    which others want yet only you may wear:
It cost me nothing, it's all I have: my need.
So wear that weed as a rose,
    Run down the garden of your years
With it as an emblem emblazoned where I rest.

THE CRONE'S LAMENT

Oh, I wish I were an orange tree,
For if I were, my breasts would be
Round as the fruit on the orange tree.
Then Time would take no toll of me
Nor my lover see this change in me
And forever more his hand could pluck
Fresh, firm fruit from a gnarled old tree.

And if he were a banana tree
Just think how useful that would be
Spring would see him growing towards me;
All Summer shew him rising to me;
Autumn would be our yielding;
And winter only our withdrawing—
If my love were a banana tree.

(*Translated from the Spanish*)

SNAPSHOT

Autumn like a pheasant's tail
   lifts over the hedge.

An old man sits in a deckchair
A paperbacked novel on his knees
                           not reading;

His worried wife forks
feebly round her border of michaelmas daisies;
                           not hoping.

Along the lane, a small girl with a pink bow
Runs home looking as contained as an apple;
                           not knowing.

A labourer pushes his bicycle up the hill
Passing beneath the copper pavilion of beech;
                           not seeing.

A poet walks through the village
And like a pickpocket possesses each
                           not belonging.

AIR RAID

Like skulls with all their fears still there
The houses squat around the square,
And through their broken windows stare
Into each other, with fixed despair.

In the hall at No. 21
Where my aunt received anyone who was somebody,
A white glove like a severed hand lies on the floor.
Her 'phone rings; but nobody answers her trunk call
      from Hades
To tell Stone where Mr. Ronald sits
At dinner—between two corsaged, safe ladies.

Now rats are residents at Embassies,
Cockroaches call, and mice are prodigal:
This war does more than spoil her Season
It's quite upset her Peke's poor reason.

And now the drunken staircase climbs the peeling walls
Into the salon where bats bleat madrigals.
Across the hearth two marble cupids sprawl.
Dust settles quietly, inheriting it all.

STROPE AND ANTI-STROPE
AT BAKERLOO

With the vision of the blind
    I see the neap-tide of spring
Move in its deep
      groin of sleep
           till as a powered wave it flings its spray
Onto the rocks, then ebbs, then falls away,
    leaving its fleece of flowers
As lilac or as lavender behind
    then as heather or as ling
The fingering surf of spring creeps
    to an old wall where as wistaria it weeps tears of
        mauve disarray
For the wind to tidy all away
    as the rain shears this fleece of flowers
with the clumsiness of thunder showers.

With the vision of the blind I see
But cannot see,
    for up and down this city street
I walk on tired tethered feet
    and with a sad persistent tread
Follow the crowds of the unburied dead
Into the Tube's anatomy
As it devours me
    into the soiled sweat and heat
Till I'm digested as soiled meat
    and packed within its bowels I'm led
Through busy labyrinths of the dead.

With the vision of the blind I see
    the earth excited with leaf and with labour
There,
    where
        the plough turns the furrow
And the belly of my fields lie fit for the harrow
    and the lumbersome corn drill parades
And the seed falls back to its secrecy
    and in blind need gives brief succour
To the earth which thirsts for
    that which is all hunger.
            Are our small eyes so shallow
Because our hearts are fallow?
    Oh! whose hand can hold the spade
And sow our eyes into each others hearts again
    till the ghost we are, is laid?

With all the callousness of fixed despair
We with marked indifference stare
    at the bunks where the bombed-out keep
Their rags of dreams in soiled sleep.
    And on a bench a couple lie quite dead,
I lift my hat. The lovers move. It was ecstasy instead. . . .
A faux pas; pardonable; compare
Love with death and there
    is little difference as they creep
Into the grave or bed of sleep.

IMPROMPTU FOR A CHILD

Like little clouds on a green sky, my sheep
Graze within their innocence of sleep

With powered flanks my arab horse
Burns like a hill of autumn gorse;

And down the lane the slow cows pass
From dreams of hay to dreams of grass.

This Earth has feet, here clay can walk,
The old elms speak, their blind leaves talk.

AMO ERGO SUM

CHOIR
>Now let us sing gaily
>>Ave Maria!
>And may the Holy Virgin
>Who was the Mother of Jesus
>Pray that these two children
>May live together happily
>For Faith releases Gaiety
>As Marriage does true Chastity
>>Ave Maria!

SOPRANO
>See how the rising sun
>Overthrows the heavy night
>And where black shadows hung
>There reveals a rose, a rose so pure and white,
>>Thus did Jesus bring
>>To the blind world of man
>That faith which is their sight
>And love that is their light.

TENOR
>As mountain streams
>>find one another
>Till they are both merged
>>there—in a broad peaceful river
>As it flows to the sea
>>and in it
>>are lost forever,

So those who love
    seek one another
But when they are joined
    here—to Christ's love, oh so tender
      yet through Him
    they love for ever.

DUET

    These two are not two
    Love has made them one
            Amo Ergo Sum!
    And by its mystery
    Each is no less but more
            Amo Ergo Sum!
    For to love is to be
    And in loving Him, I love thee,
            Amo Ergo Sum!

OMNES

    Per vitam Domini
      Spes nobis cantavit,
    Per fidem Domini
      Lux diem novavit
    Per mortem Domini
      Mors mortem fugavit,
    Amen!

*(Sung at the wedding of the Earl and Countess of Harewood
and set by Benjamin Britten)*

THE
SOLITUDES

RONALD DUNCAN

FABER AND FABER

24 Russell Square

London

First published in mcmlx
by Faber and Faber Limited
24 Russell Square London W.C.1
Printed in Great Britain by
Latimer Trend & Co Ltd Plymouth